Prayers for the Journey Vol. II

By

Audrey C. Jackson

Prayers for the Journey
Vol. II

Cover Art and Design by Mary Fusco.

Dedication:

This book of prayers is humbly dedicated to all who love to pray.

Table of Contents

Scriptural Prayers

Romans 12 Prayer

Heavenly Father, in view of your mercy, I offer you my body as a living sacrifice, holy and acceptable—this is my true and proper worship to you. Help me not to conform to the pattern of this world, but to be transformed by the renewing of my mind. Then I will be able to test and approve what your will is—your good, pleasing and perfect will.

Help me not to think of myself more highly than I ought; to be honest in evaluating and measuring myself by the faith you have given me. Show me how to esteem others more than myself. Thank you, Lord for the different gifts of grace you give us in the body of Christ to enable us to do all things well. We prophesy in proportion to the faith you give us, and we serve with a willing heart. Bless us as we teach and exhort according to your word. Thank you, Lord that we give liberally, we lead with diligence and we show mercy with cheerfulness.

Lord, bless me to love others sincerely without hypocrisy. Teach me to abhor what is evil and to cling to what is good. Teach me to be kind and loving to others and to honor them above myself. May I never lack zeal but keep my spiritual fervor in serving you. Help me to rejoice in hope, be patient through tribulations and faithful in prayer as I practice hospitality and give to the saints who are in need.

Teach me to bless and pray for those who curse and persecute me, to rejoice with those who rejoice and weep with those who weep. Give me a mindset to live in harmony with others, to not be proud and conceited but to associate with all types of people.

I will not repay anyone evil for evil; I will be careful to do what is right and honorable in the sight of everyone. I will not give place to wrath but will wait on you Lord for you said, "Vengeance is mine." Therefore, with the help of Christ Jesus I will live peacefully with all people. If my enemy is hungry, I will feed him; if he is thirsty, I will give him something to drink. In doing this, I will overcome evil with good. In the name of Jesus, Amen.

Ephesians Prayer

Blessed be the God and Father of our Lord Jesus Christ, who has blessed us with every spiritual blessing in the heavenly places because we are united in Christ. You accomplished this when you raised Christ from the dead and seated him at your right hand in the heavenly places. Thank you, God, for also raising us up with Christ (the body) so that your manifold wisdom might now be made known through the church to the rulers and authorities in the heavenly places.

For our struggle is not against flesh and blood, but against the rulers, against the authorities, against the powers of this dark world, against the spiritual forces of evil in the heavenly realms. Therefore, we wear the whole armor of God so we are able to take our stand against the devil's schemes, and when we have done all, we will still stand!

God of our Lord Jesus Christ, please give us spiritual wisdom and insight so that we might grow in our knowledge of you. Lord, flood our hearts with light so that we will understand what we are called to do. We pray that we believers will come to understand the incredible greatness of your power for us which is the same mighty power that raised Christ from the dead.

Ephesians 1:3, 20, 2:6; 3:10; 6:12-13; 1:17-19

My Life in Christ Prayer

Heavenly Father, I thank you that I have been raised to a new life with Christ Jesus and I seek those things which are above, where he sits in the place of honor at your right hand. My mind and thoughts are on those kingdom things and not on earthly things for I died to self and my life is now in Christ. I put to death the sinful, worldly things lurking within me and I want nothing to do with sexual immorality, impurity, lust, or greed.

I put on my new nature and renew my mind as I learn to know you, my Creator and become like you. I thank you God that in my new life, nationality doesn't matter, gender doesn't matter and position doesn't matter; all that matter is Jesus Christ and he lives in me.

Lord, you chose me to be a part of your kingdom so I must now become more Christ-like as I demonstrate tenderhearted mercy, kindness, humility, gentleness, and patience. I must overlook other's faults and forgive anyone who may offend me. I remember that you forgave me, so I must forgive others. Above all I cover myself with love because that is what binds us all together in perfect harmony. I let the peace that comes from you rule in my heart since as members of one body I am called to live in peace and to be always thankful.

This message about Christ in all his richness fills my life and I teach and counsel others with all the wisdom he gives me. I sing psalms and hymns and spiritual songs with a thankful heart; realizing that whatever I do or say, I must do it as a representative of the Lord Jesus, giving thanks always to you, God the Father.

Lord, I will work willingly at whatever you give me to do as though I am working for you and not for people. I realize you are the one who will reward me for my service. Thank you for hearing me. Amen.

Colossians 3:1-5, 10-17, 24

Your Word is Light

(Based on Psalms 119)

Your word, O Lord, is a lamp to guide my feet and a light on my path. I am blessed when I stay on course and walk the road revealed by you. Don't let me go off on my own following after a false light.

Lord, guide my steps by your word so I will not be overcome by evil. Provide me with insight and a discerning mind that only comes from your word. Teach me good judgment. Help me to abandon my shameful ways. Open my eyes to see the wonderful truth in your instructions.

The entrance of your word gives light; it gives understanding to the ordinary person. I rejoice in your word like one who discovers a great treasure. Your word pleases me; from it I obtain wise advice and counsel. I have hidden your word in my heart that I might not sin against you.

I love that the very essence of your word is truth and will stand forever. All your commands are true. I hate and abhor all falsehood but I love your word and will obey your decrees. How sweet are your word to my taste; sweeter than honey to my mouth!

Your word comforts me just as you promised; it prompts praise to flow from my lips. My tongue sings your words; all your commands are righteous and good. As my soul lives, it will praise you.

Forever O Lord, your eternal word is settled in and stands firm in heaven. Your faithfulness extends to every generation.

Psalm 119:3, 8, 11, 18, 24, 39, 66, 76, 89, 90, 103, 105, 130, 133, 151, 160, 162, 163, 169, 171, 172, 175

Affirmation Prayer

Thank you, Lord that I dwell in the secret place of you the Most High and I rest under the wings of your protection. You are my defender and protector; in you I trust. You keep me safe from all hidden dangers; you deliver me from the enemy's plans and schemes.

I thank you God that you are cleansing me from secret sins; they have no place in me. I confess my sins and faults and I receive your forgiveness. I do not hold grudges because I forgive other as I have been forgiven. I have the mind of Christ and I will not be tormented by impure, fearful, negative or sinful thoughts which are lies of the enemy. I take every thought captive and replace it with a godly and holy word of scripture.

In the name of Jesus, I resist lying thoughts and command lying spirits to be gone from my mind. I proclaim that God has given me a sound mind. I will not entertain confusion but live in clarity as I am strong in you Lord and in the power of your might! I command the spirit of fear and all spirits associated with fear to leave now and not return. I cast you out!

Lord, as your word says, I will not be anxious about anything, instead I will take my concerns to you in prayer. I proclaim that your peace will guard my heart and mind as I live and breathe in you. Christ Jesus, you keep me in perfect peace because my mind is stayed on you. Therefore, I will think things that are worthy of praise, things that are true, honorable, pure, right, and kind. Thank you, Lord for hearing my prayer. Amen!

Psalm 91:1-3, 1John 1:9, Matt. 6:14-15, Phil 2:5, 2 Cor. 10:3-5,
2 Tim 1:7, Eph. 6:10, Phil. 4:6-8, Isaiah 26:3

Wisdom

(Based on Proverbs 3)

Lord, I will not forget your teachings, they are entrenched in my heart prolonging my life and bringing me peace and prosperity. I will keep your attributes of love, mercy, kindness, and truth in the center of my heart as they are very important to me. These virtues will give me favor and a good name in your sight and in the sight of mankind.

I trust you Lord with all my heart and I do not rely on my own understanding. In everything I do, I will put you first, seeking your will in all situations so you can show me the right path to take. I will not be wise or impressed with my own wisdom; I will seek your wisdom which comes from above. I fear you and shun evil as it brings health and healing to my body and nourishment to my bones.

I honor you Lord with all the wealth that I am in possession of, giving you the first and the best so that my blessings will overflow. Lord, you discipline me because you love me so I will not complain or resent your corrections even though it doesn't feel good.

I am blessed to find wisdom and to acquire understanding; for wisdom is more profitable than silver and yields better returns than gold. Wisdom is more precious than rubies and nothing I desire can compare with her. Long life is in her right hand; in her left hand are riches and honor. Her ways are pleasant and all her paths are peace. She is a tree of life to all who embrace and hold her tightly.

I will not let go of sound wisdom and understanding; they will always be a part of me. They are life for my soul and an adornment to grace my outer self. Lord, thank you for your wisdom and for giving me understanding.

Prayer of Repentance

(Daniel 9:4-19)

O Lord, you are a great and awesome God! You always fulfill your covenant and keep your promises of unfailing love to those who love you and obey your commands. But we as a people have sinned and done wrong. We have rebelled against you and scorned your commands and regulations. We have refused to listen to your servants the prophets, who spoke with your authority to our leaders and ancestors and to all the people of the land.

Lord, you have done everything right, but all we have to show for our lives is guilt and shame, this is true of all of us. O LORD, we and our leaders, and our ancestors are covered with shame because we have sinned against you. We've been exposed in our shame, all of us— before the whole world. And we deserve it. Your compassion is our only hope, since in our rebellion we've forfeited our rights.

But God you are merciful and forgiving, even though we have rebelled against you. We paid no attention to you when you told us how to live, the clear teaching that came through your servants the prophets. All of us ignored what you said. We defied your instructions and did what we pleased. And now we're paying for it.

We have not obeyed you, for we have not followed the instructions you gave us through your servants. All of us have disobeyed your instruction and turned away, refusing to listen to your voice.

So now we are suffering the consequences of our rebellion. You have kept your word and done to us and our leaders exactly as you warned. Yet even now we have refused to seek mercy from you Lord and we have not turned from our sins and recognized your truth. Therefore, you have brought upon us the disaster you prepared. You are right to do all of these things, for we did not obey you.

O Lord our God, you brought lasting honor to your name by rescuing and delivering your people from numerous situations in great displays of power.

We have sinned and are full of wickedness, but we call on your mercy. Lord, please turn your furious anger away from us, as a result of our sins and the sins of our ancestors.

O my God, please listen to my prayer! Listen as I plead. For your own sake, Lord, smile again on our nation. O my God, incline your ear and hear; open your eyes and see our condition. We make this plea, not because we deserve help, but because of your mercy.

O Lord, hear. O Lord, forgive. O Lord, listen and act! For your own sake, do not delay, for your people are called by your name!

Fearfully & Wonderfully Made

(Based on Psalm 139)

Lord God, you alone know all about me; you examine my heart and know all that I think and do. You know and understand my thoughts even from afar. You know what I am going to say even before I say it. Your presence goes before me and at the same time you are following me. This kind of knowledge is too wonderful for me, too great for me to understand!

If I wanted to escape from your Spirit, from your very presence, where would I go? If I go up to heaven, you are there; if I go down to the grave, you are there. If I ask the darkness to hide me, and the light around me to become night, but even in darkness I cannot hide from you. To you the night shines as bright as day. Darkness and light are the same to you!

You know my innermost being because you designed and created me. You made all the delicate, inner parts of my body and knit me together in my mother's womb. Thank you for making me so wonderfully complex! I praise you because I am fearfully and wonderfully made; your works are marvelous, and my soul knows it very well. Nothing pertaining to me was hidden from you as I was being made. You saw my substance before it was formed yet every day of my life was recorded in your book; every moment was laid out before a single day had passed.

O God, how precious and enumerable are your thoughts about me. You stay with me even when I walk away from you. I don't understand it but I thank you with all my being. Now O God, search my heart; test me and know my anxious thoughts. Point out anything in me that offends you and lead me along the path of everlasting life. Amen

Psalm 8 Prayer

O Lord, my Lord, how excellent you are; how majestic and glorious is your name in all the earth. Your glory is magnificent, it covers the heavens! You are so wonderful and more glorious then I could ever imagine!

From the lips of children and infants, you have called forth your praise so as to silence your enemy and avenger.

When I consider and look at the heavens that you created, I am in awe of the wonderful works of your very fingers. How you ordained the moon and the stars and set them in their place is beyond my comprehension!

Lord, you made humans and that means me, in your image, and you made us a little lower than yourself and then placed your glory and honor on us. You not only loved and cared for us, you also gave us dominion over the works of your hands. We were given authority and ruler ship over all the animals of the fields, bird of the air and fish of the sea. WOW!

Again, I can only say, O Lord, my Lord, how excellent and majestic you are in all the earth, in all the earth, in all the earth! Amen.

Anguish of the Soul

(Psalm 77)

Lord, I cried out to you for help; I needed you to hear me because I was in trouble. All night long I prayed to you with uplifted hands toward heaven, but my soul was not comforted. When I think of you, I am over whelmed with my longing for your help. I am unable to sleep and have difficulty praying. I think back over my life during happier times and wonder what happened!

Have you rejected me Lord? Did I lose your favor? Have you withdrawn your love from me? Lord, what happened to your promises and have you forgotten to be merciful? Did you close the door on your compassion?

Then it came to me all the wonderful things you have done for me, the miracles of past years. I meditated on each one of those mighty deeds and your goodness flooded my soul! Thank you for allowing me to recall and remember these events.

Oh God, your ways are holy. There is no god as mighty as you. You are the God who performs miracles, who displays awesome power among the people.

Thank you, Lord for my awakening!

Personal Prayers

Healing Prayer

Lord God, your word said Jesus was wounded for my transgressions and bruised for my iniquities and by his stripes I am healed! I pray for increased faith in that word to heal and restore my body to full restoration. I pray for your word to penetrate my heart for out of it springs life and healing to my entire body. Help me to guard my heart from doubt and unbelief. (Prov. 4:21-23)

The word in 1 Peter 2:24 says "by whose stripes I was healed;" therefore, I call forth that which you have already provided. I receive your healing power as I meditate on your word and speak truth to my mind and body. It is reaching deep inside me to kill off any germs and diseases that may have gained an entry.

I speak life to each one of my organs; you will function in the manner God intended you to. I declare that my organs are healthy and made whole in the name of Jesus! I will not tolerate any symptoms of illness in my body. I take authority over them and tell them to leave my body in the name of Jesus and not return!

Thank you, dear Lord for healing and continued good health. I am grateful for the sacrifice of your own body so that my body can be healed. Bless me to be a vessel for your glory!

In the name of Jesus, I pray! Amen.

Speak to the Mountain

Lord God, you told us in your word that we could speak to the mountain in faith and it would be moved (Mark 11:23). I want to be obedient to you and your word but I find myself doing just the opposite; speaking negatively about my circumstances rather than positively.

Please forgive me for my doubt and unbelief. Help me to call those things that are not as though they were (Rom. 4:17). I desire to speak life sustaining things about myself and others, so please guard my tongue. Make real to me the scripture that says, *Death and life are in the power of my tongue* (Prov. 18:21). I will speak healing to my body in the name of Jesus until I receive the manifestation of it! (1 Peter 2:24)

Lord, open my ears to hear your word and then to speak them. Don't let the enemy steal the word from me as they are life and healing to my whole body. Guard my heart for out of it determines the course of my life. Remove from me anything that hinders my walk with you.

I know I am to renew my mind so my thinking aligns with the mind of Christ. Remind me take capture all negative thoughts and lies and make them obedient to Christ (2 Cor. 10:5). Whenever these unwelcome thoughts enter my mind, I will replace them with your word.

I declare that I will read and meditate on those things that are essential to my well-being; things that are true, honorable, pure, lovely, and a good report. I will think on those things that are excellent and worthy of praise. As I put these things into practice, I expect to be one with the God of peace. (Phil. 4:8-9).

Thank you, Lord! In the name of Jesus, I pray.

Spiritual Gifts

Lord God, your word said that each person in the body of Christ has been given spiritual gifts or special abilities that demonstrate your power. I thank you Holy Spirit for imparting these marvelous gifts to me for the benefit of the body of Christ. The spiritual gifts listed in 1 Corinthians 12 are essential for me in carrying out that principle.

You said I should earnestly desire spiritual gifts, but mostly I need to understand and appreciate that all spiritual gifts must function in love. These gifts are nothing if I do not have love in my heart for others. Lord, I pray to operate in spiritual gifts and to follow the path of love.

I expect and actively welcome the gifts of the Holy Spirit to flow through me as I minister and serve in the kingdom of God. Open the eyes of my heart so I will know the gifts you desire to bless me with. Give me the boldness to step out and minister in those gifts.

Lord, I am your masterpiece created in Christ Jesus for good works that you intend for me to carry out. That includes flowing in spiritual gifts in a way that helps others and brings glory to your name. If I speak a word of prophecy, enable me to do it in a way that strengthens, encourages, or comforts the church. If I receive a message to give in tongues, may I deliver it with boldness and an expectation that I, or someone else, will interpret it to bless the body.

If I receive a word of knowledge or a word of wisdom, help me to give that word in a way that conveys your love to the person. If the gift of healing or the gift to perform miracles flow through me, may I always be aware that the power to do this comes from you, Holy Spirit.

Surely, I will need the gift of discerning of spirits and the gift of faith in my walk. Lord, I am grateful for whatever gift(s) you endow me with and use me for; and I promise to operate in those gifts for your glory. In the name of Jesus, I pray. Amen.

Gift of Life

Thank you, Lord for creating me in your image, making me a spirit being.

Thank you for my:

Body which is fearfully and wonderfully made.
Soul which contains the breath of life.
Spirit which communes with you, hearing what you have to say.
Mind with its intellect, creativity, and godly thoughts.
Emotions that allow me to feel love, joy, peace, compassion and mercy.
Will in that you allow me to choose blessings or curses, life or death, heaven or hell.
Eyes which can see your beauty and not the ugliness of the evil one.
Ears that hear your word and hear the sweet sound of music flowing from the throne.
Voice which speaks praises to you and exhorts and encourages others.
Nose which smells your sweet aroma and not the stench of death and defilement.
Tongue which can taste the sweetness of your word and spit out the root of bitterness.
Hands which allow me to clap in praise to you as well as to impart a healing to someone.
Legs and feet which takes me to places you desire me to go.
Heart to love all those I encounter.
Energy that flows through my body strengthening me.
Spiritual gifts that empower me to minister to others.

I am forever grateful!

Woman of Destiny

Thank you, Lord that you made me a woman of destiny, created in Christ Jesus to do good works in your kingdom. I am blessed with every spiritual blessing in the heavenly places in Christ Jesus where I am seated.

Lord, I am in awe of how you made all the delicate inner parts of my body and put them together in my mother's womb. Your word says I am fearfully and wonderfully made! Thank you for making me so amazingly intricate, your workmanship is incredible. You knew me before you formed me in my mother's womb; before I was born you set me apart for the calling you have on my life. You said I am a chosen vessel, a royal priest, holy, and peculiar.

I praise you because you called me out of darkness and put me into your marvelous light! Thank you that you redeemed my life from the pit and crowned me with love and compassion. You said that I am a crown of splendor, a royal diadem in your hand. The precious jewels in my crown sparkle with the light of Jesus that shines from within me, identifying me as a vessel of love!

Oh Lord, how precious are your thoughts to me! I treasure each word of wisdom you give me because nothing compares to it. You have given me the tongue of the learned so I know how to speak a word in season to the weary. You awaken me each morning and open my ears to listen like one being instructed. I anxiously wait to hear from you, so Speak Lord!

I am so grateful to you Lord for how you have sustained me through all the trials and tests that came my way. They did not, nor will they, defeat me. Hallelujah! I am an over-comer! I will persevere and obtain the crown of life and crown of righteousness that you promised to those who love you. Lord God, I praise you, I honor you, and I love you. In the name of Jesus, I pray!

Ephesians 1:3, 2:6, Psalm 139:13-14, 1 Peter 2:9, Psalm 103:4, Isaiah 62:3, Zechariah 9:16, Proverb 3:15, Isaiah 50:4-5, James 1:12, 2 Timothy 4:8

Purpose Driven

Thank you, Lord that you instilled in me a determination to be purpose driven; seeking always to please you. My desire is to dedicate my life to you in service to the kingdom of God.

I thank you for the plans you have for me as they are plans to prosper me and not to harm me. Your plans give me a hope and a future. Lord, I will be strong and courageous and do what you called me to do. I will not be afraid or discouraged for you are with me wherever I go and whatever I do. You are my strong fortress and my ever-present help in time of trouble.

My purpose in life is to do your will, so I declare that I am purpose driven as I seek your presence and meditate on your word. I am purpose driven as I seek your spiritual wisdom and understanding so I may grow in my knowledge of you. I am purpose driven as demonstrated by how I love my sisters and brothers in Christ.

I am purpose driven as I walk in obedience to your word. I am purpose driven as I go into the highways and byways telling everyone how great you are, and how you love them and want them to believe on your Son Jesus.

I praise you Lord with all my heart. I sing praises to your name, O Lord as I bow before you in humble adoration for your faithfulness and love to me. You are an Awesome God! Awesome God! Awesome God! Amen.

Seeking the Presence of the Lord

Lord God, I praise you with all my heart, all my innermost being praises your name. I enter into your gates with thanksgiving and into your courts with praise. You are El Elyon, God Most High; El Shaddai, the All Sufficient One!

My desire is to stay in your presence, beholding your beauty and holiness. Early in the morning I will seek you. I will meditate on you in the night watches. I will call on your name because you are my God and I am your beloved. Your word says if I call you, you will answer, I will be found by you.

I am calling on you now to tell you my soul thirsts for you, O God. My flesh longs for you. Only you can satisfy this longing in my heart. Fill me with your love. Fill me with your joy. Fill me with your shalom peace. Saturate me with your manifested presence.

As I bask in your love and splendor, I feel your arms embracing me in a warm, comforting hug. Your touch means everything to me. It is what I need and desire; it is what I yearn for. Show me your glory; I want to behold your glory.

Lord God, I thank you for my very existence, for the person you made me to be. I thank you for being my all Sufficient One. You supply everything I need because you are Jehovah Jireh, my provider. You care for me in such a tender way. I love you Lord and I bless your holy name.

In the name of Jesus, I pray this prayer. Amen.

Prayer for Revelation Knowledge

Lord God, I pray that you would give me the spirit of wisdom and revelation in the knowledge of you, so that I may know you better. I pray that my heart be flooded with light so that I may know and understand the hope you have given to those you called. I also pray to understand the incredible greatness of your power for us who believe in you. Your word says this is the same mighty power that raised Christ from the dead and seated him in the place of honor at your right hand in the heavenly realms.

Open my spiritual eyes and ears to receive all that you have for me. Reveal yourself to me in a new way. As you speak to me in dreams and visions, help me to remember and give me an understanding and interpretation of them. I ask that you remove anything that hinders me from clearly hearing and seeing you. Teach me what you want me to know and believe as I grow in my journey with you. Help me to discern and recognize the signs you give your Church when you are shifting and moving in a new direction.

Lord, I am grateful to you for the gifts you have given me so that I am a blessing to your Body. I give you all praise, honor and glory, because you are able to accomplish infinitely more than I might ask or think through your mighty power at work within me.

It is in the precious name of Jesus, I pray. Amen.

There is no Condemnation

Lord, there are times when I feel downcast and sadden, so unworthy of anything. At times, my heart is heavy with feelings of rejection. I feel as though I am deteriorating in all areas of my life; not pleasing to you and not pleasing to myself. This state of mind is discouraging and depressing causing me to belittle myself; and denigrating others. In this state, I find some comfort in lashing out and condemning others, finding flaws and faults in them.

Lord, my brokenness, my ailing heart, and my open wounds are pulling me down into darkness. Grab hold of my hand and pull me up from my abyss. Holy Spirit, open the eyes of my spirit so I can hear you again. I need your truth to quash the lies I have believed about myself.

Your word says in Romans 8:1 that there is no condemnation to those that belong to Christ Jesus, who do not walk according to the flesh but according to the Spirit. Refresh me with your life given power so I can truly believe your word. Help me to not indulge in negative thinking and to replace them with thoughts that are pleasing to you and edifying to me.

Forgive me for not fully believing your word. Forgive me for the things I have said about myself and other people. Help me to love myself as you love me which is unconditional. Thank you, for I am now convinced that nothing can separate me from your love that is in Christ Jesus my Lord. I am accepted in the beloved! Amen.

Sexual Abuse

Heavenly Father, I am your child crying out to you because you are a loving and merciful God and I need you right now.

Lord, I am hurting from the effects of sexual abuse and associated emotional pain and suffering. This trauma runs deep within me; it affects every aspect of my being. To make matters worse, I felt I had done something to cause the attack. I now recognize that was a lie from the devil causing me to feel shame and guilt unnecessarily. Also, I felt betrayed because the person who assaulted me was someone I trusted.

I refuse to accept the blame for any part of what happened to me; I was victimized! I did not bring this assault on myself and I no longer believe the lies of the enemy whispering to me that it was my fault. My body, which you made fearfully and wonderfully just for me, was forcefully invaded without my consent. My virginity and innocence were stolen from me; my trust was hijacked!

Lord, does the person who did this know the extent of their sin against me and the damage it caused that can only be reversed by you? I pray that you will convict them of their immoral and wicked action so they can repent.

I want to be made whole again so I release all feelings of bitterness, hatred and anger in the name of Jesus. I declare these feelings will no longer control my life. I forgive my abuser(s), not to let them off the hook, but because forgiveness will allow me to heal. My abuser(s) will still have to answer to you, the righteous Judge.

Lord, thank you for the healing and restoration of my body and emotions. Your healing balm of Gilead is both soothing and comforting to me. As I reflect on your goodness, I receive your heavenly blessings and bask in your glory! I declare that I am healed and made whole in the name of Jesus! Hallelujah, and Amen!

Help My Unbelief

Lord, you said in your word that all things are possible to those who believe. I do believe, but help my unbelief! Sometimes the circumstances are so overwhelming and overpowering that it makes me struggle to believe anything but what I see in the natural. It is particularly difficult when the situation or condition continues for an extended period of time.

I want to believe your promises, but I admit I still have unbelief in some areas. Help me to believe your word in 2 Cor. 4:18 that says, to not look at the problems but fix my eyes on what is unseen, since what is seen is temporary, but the unseen is eternal and lasting.

Jesus, when the men told Jairus that his daughter was dead, you spoke to him and said, "do not be afraid; only believe." The circumstances were bad and were made worse by the delay of the woman with the issue of blood seeking your help. You wanted him to hear you and not the report of what was in the natural. He believed you and you raised his daughter from the dead!

Lord, help me to only hear you and your promises; enable me to see in the spiritual realm and not focus on the natural. Open the eyes of my heart; I want to see you. Help me to wait on you no matter how long it takes because your promises are Yes, and Amen!

Forgiveness

Lord God, my heart is heavy, I am wrestling with offense from someone close who is seemingly unaware of their trespass against me. I need your help to process the fallout of the offense and to heal the hurt inflicted by them. Jesus, I am crying out to you because I know you too experienced the sting of offense many times during your time on earth.

Lord, why is it that people lash out and hurt other people? What are the underlying issues that allow this behavior? Is it selfishness; is it control, is it jealousy? Are they hurt themselves?

Lord God, I pray that you touch the heart of the one who caused the offense and heal whatever wounds they may have. Bring them to the point of self-awareness and remorse that would allow them to cry out to you for healing and then make an effort to mend their past actions.

Speak to my heart Lord and remind me that I must continue to forgive as I am forgiven. I realize your word says that offense is one of the strategies of the enemy to wreak relationships. Give me a pure heart toward them so there is nothing in me that opens the door to the enemy.

I just needed to talk to you about my feelings realizing you would understand and enable me to process the effects of the offense. Help me to not receive an offense in the future, to not let it land at my door. I do forgive because I will not allow bitterness to take root in me. I am your beloved child who chooses to stay on the path of righteousness.

Thank you for listening to me and allowing me to arrive at where I needed to be, right in the center of your will. Amen.

Restful Sleep

In the name of Jesus, I bind the enemy and forbid him from interfering with my sleep in any way. I loose the atmosphere of peace and serenity in my home and in my bedroom. Lord God, I will have no fear when I lie down to sleep for you are with me.

I rest in the knowledge that I am the beloved child of the Most High God; and I am promised sweet sleep which I now claim in the name of Jesus (Prov. 3:24). My body will rest secure in the knowledge of my position in Christ where I am seated in the heavenly realm.

Lord, you are my refuge and fortress, my God in whom I trust! Thank you for my angels who are surrounding my bed protecting and delivering me from any and all evil (Psalm 34:7).

Even as I sleep dear Lord, you are counseling me and giving me divine instructions (Psalm 16:7). My soul awaits to hear from you in visions and dreams. Thank you for sweet, restful sleep through the night and for being refreshed in the morning.

In the name of Jesus, I pray. Amen

Prosper and be in Good Health

Lord, I pray to prosper and be in good health even as my soul prospers (3 John 1:2). That is your desire for me and I receive it. You came to earth that I may have life and have it more abundantly. I want that truth to become a realty in my life.

Lord, help me to trust in you and not to depend on my own understanding knowing that you will show me the correct path to take. I will not be wise in my own eyes. My desire is to continue to be in awe of you and shun evil, which will bring health to my body and nourishment to my bones (Prov. 3:5-8). As I honor you by giving you my first and best, you promise to abundantly bless me in return.

The word says in Joshua 1:8 that if I study and meditate on your word and careful to be obedient to it; I can be prosperous and successful in all that I do. Thank you for the wisdom of your word that teaches me how to abide in you and live a discipline and fruitful life.

I pray that you will give me spiritual wisdom and insight so I may grow in my knowledge of you. Flood my heart with light so I may grasp the enormity of this wonderful life you called me to and to live it accordingly (Eph. 1:17-18). I pray to have a walk worthy of you Lord, fully pleasing you in everything I do.

May the words of my lips and the meditation of my heart be pleasing to you, O Lord; my strength and my Redeemer. (Psalm 19:14)

Prayer for Salvation

Lord Jesus, I believe that you are the son of God and that you came to earth in the flesh and died on the cross for my sins. Please come into my heart and save me from the clutches of the enemy. I receive you as my Savior, my Lord and my Master. Thank you for my eternal salvation.

The above prayer prayed in faith and believed in the heart will save you. (Romans 10:9-10)

Warfare Prayers

Freedom from Oppressive Spirits

Father God, your word says in Acts 10:38 that Jesus healed all who were oppressed by the devil for you were with him. I believe that word is still applicable for today and that I can appropriate it for myself.

I feel oppressed and over whelmed at time, so I am crying out to you to deliver me from the oppressor. Forgive me for any sins I may have committed that opened the door to the oppressor. Give me a fresh anointing of your Holy Spirit that will break every yoke and set me free.

As I seek your presence, may the healing power of Jesus Christ invade my body and lift the dark cloud over me. I pray to be led to green pastures and still waters where you are and where you will restore my soul.

Thank you for lifting this oppressive spirit and for giving me the oil of joy, and a garment of praise. Thank you that you will keep me in perfect peace as I intentionally fix my eyes and thoughts on you. I will bless you at all times; your praise will continually be in my mouth!

Now may your peace which surpasses all understanding, rest, rule and abide in me. Amen

Sexual Sin Prayer

Father God, I repent of all sexual sins that have led to a demonic stronghold in my life. I repent on behalf of my ancestors and myself who opened the door and committed sexual sins. In the name of Jesus, I renounce any generational curse that would connect me to any kind of sexual perversion. The curse is broken off me and my seed!

I renounce any emotional wounds, brokenness, or rejection that may have opened doors to rebellion in the area of sexual sin in my life. I renounce and close all doors that were opened through traumatic events. I renounce and close all doors that may have been opened through sexual abuse (rape, molestation, or incest) in infancy, adolescence, or adulthood. I renounce and sever ties to demonic spirits that may have gained entrance through these evil acts. I repent of and renounce any soul ties I have made. In the name of Jesus, I renounce all curses spoken over me, against me, or by me.

Help me Lord to renew my mind which was affected by my sexual sins. I take every thought captive to Christ that says I am under the power of the enemy. I am not a victim any longer. I am washed and cleansed by the blood of Jesus; and I will not allow myself to be open to any unholy alliances.

I willingly submit my body as a living sacrifice unto you God. I declare my loins are girded with truth and my heart is fixed on you. I will not give in to sinful desires and I will not let any part of my body become an instrument of evil.

I consider myself to be dead to the power of sin and alive to you God through Christ Jesus. Thank you, Lord for answering this prayer that is prayed in the mighty name of Jesus!

Breaking Soul Ties

Lord, please forgive me for looking to another human being to fix the need and pain inside of me. I desire to be free from any and all ungodly soul tie that I may have formed. I repent for allowing this to happen. I humbly ask you to forgive me and cleanse me of the sin of fornication and wrong alliance that knitted us together in an ungodly manner. I acknowledge it as sin and ask you to help me forsake it completely in the name of Jesus.

In Jesus' mighty name, I sever any and all ungodly soul ties between myself and [say the NAME or NAMES] created by sexual acts or any other type of behavior. I renounce every wrong agreement that caused a birthing of these ungodly soul ties. Lord, I choose now to realign my thinking so that it is in compliance with your will. I have the mind of Christ and my eye is fixed on you.

By the authority of the name of the Lord Jesus Christ, I break the power of any and all ungodly unions, covenants, or contracts made by me or someone else on my behalf. I now command any and all demons which may have come into me by ungodly soul ties or any other sin to leave me at once, never to return.

Abba Father, in Jesus' mighty name, I ask you to shut and seal any doorways of demonic access so there is no possible right of entry through which satan can trouble me or my family ever again.

I now invite Holy Spirit to come in and dwell in every part of me and to fill and sanctify all places where the enemy resided. Cleanse me with the blood of Jesus and I will be clean. I thank you for doing this in Jesus' mighty name. Amen.

Prayer of Protection

My Lord and my God, I acknowledge your presence in this room and in my life. You are the only omniscient (all knowing), omnipotent (all powerful), and omnipresent (all present) God. I am dependent upon you for apart from you I can do nothing.

I stand upon the truth that all authority in heaven and earth has been given to Jesus Christ, and because I am in Christ, I share that authority. I pray for your complete protection as I go forward learning about this spiritual conflict and warring in the spiritual realm the way you have ordained for me. In Jesus' name, Amen.

Breaking Generational
Iniquities & Bondages

Father God, I come to you in the name and power of your son, Jesus Christ. I repent of my sins and the sins of my ancestors that allowed iniquities and bondages in our family. Please forgive us for opening the door to the enemy and becoming enslaved to him. Thank you, Jesus that you disarmed the evil powers and authorities at the cross and made a spectacle of them (Col.2:15).

In the name of Jesus, I bind the strongman; and I loose and reclaim every bit of joy, peace, blessings, material and spiritual possession he has stolen from me. I do this in the name of Jesus Christ who has given me the keys and authority to do so.

I renounce every sin and every spirit that accompanies that sin, and I break the hold that sin had on me and my family members. I renounce every sinful and ungodly attitude, way of thinking, belief, and behavior that I have learned.

I break generational curses and sicknesses that have occurred in my family. They have no more effect upon me or any member of my family. I break the power and effect of harsh words or curses spoken about me, to me, or by me. I sever any and all ungodly soul ties.

I am grateful that the blood of Jesus has power to demolish all strongholds and bondages from my mind, spirit and body. I break every yoke and bondage from my past and the past of my ancestors, and I sever those ties through the power of the blood of Jesus.

I declare that I and my family are now free from the enemy's grip. Everything that the enemy has stolen will be restored to me. I am healed and set free in Jesus' name.

Lord, I choose to forgive all those who have wronged me. I do this because I recognize that you have forgiven me, so I too must walk in forgiveness. Help me Holy Spirit to get rid of all bitterness, anger, and resentment.

Heal the pain and damage caused by the attacks of satan on me and my family. Open my eyes to see the enemy's stronghold, and prompt me to use the sword of the Spirit to stand against him.

Lord, I thank you for the victory and I ask that you fill me afresh and anew with the fullness of the Holy Spirit. I want to live in him and be guided by him. I pray this prayer in the name of Jesus Christ. Amen.

Breaking Word Curses

In the name of Jesus, I break every word curse spoken about me, or to me. I take every word curse captive that has been spoken over me or that I spoke over myself. I break the power of those curses and loose their effects on me. I cancel every devilish assignment from the enemy and I call forth blessings to fall in its place. I thank you Jesus that you became a curse for me and I now dwell in your righteousness.

Breaking Generational Curses

In the name of Jesus, I repent of all the sins of my ancestors to the 4th generation as well as those sins committed by me. I renounce the sins of each generation and break their hold on me and my family. I cancel every assignment of the enemy and remove any right of the demonic to afflict us. I now call forth my righteous inheritance and the blessings of those generations.

Breaking Soul Ties

I plead the blood of Jesus to stand between me and (name of the person) to separate the "one flesh" union. I send back to him/her everything that I have taken from him/her in the one flesh union and I call back to me everything that I gave him/her in the one flesh union. I now sever all ties and close the doors that were opened by me. I thank you Jesus for restoring my soul and making me whole again.

Spiritual Cleansing of Home and Business

Lord God, thank you for this beautiful establishment that you have entrusted to us. We claim this home/business as a place of spiritual safety and refuge. Our prayer is that you will protect us from any attacks of the enemy.

In the name of Jesus, we renounce and cancel all demonic assignments directed against this place or its occupants. We command every evil spirit claiming ground in this place based on activity of past occupants to leave and never return. Lord God, we ask that you post your holy angels all around this dwelling repelling all evil spirits.

May all who enters our doors be blessed of the Lord! In the name of Jesus, I pray this prayer. Amen.

Spiritual Authority Prayer

Father God, I thank you that you have given all authority in heaven and on earth to Jesus Christ who has delegated this authority to his church. Lord, help us all to walk in the authority you have given us; and to know in particular that we have authority to trample on serpents and scorpions and to overcome all the power of the enemy.

Thank you for giving me authority and power in the ministry of healing and deliverance where the need is so great. I desire to bring release to those who are oppressed and to lay hands on the sick and see them recover for your glory.

With the authority you have given me, I rebuke sickness in my own body and command any evil spirits to leave in the name of Jesus! I break every generational curse off me, and every spirit of infirmity and affliction must leave now!

Thank you, Lord for increasing boldness and faith in me to do all you have commanded me to do and to bring this same revelation and release to others. In the precious name of Jesus, I pray.

Renouncing Sins of Ancestors

I repent and renounce all the sins of my ancestors as well as those sins committed by me. I now sever all ties and close the doors that were opened by my ancestors as well as myself. I have been delivered from the domain of darkness and am in the kingdom of God. Every curse placed on me was broken when Christ became a curse for me.

I am blessed with every spiritual blessing in the heavenly places in Christ as I am now seated with him in the heavenly places far above all principalities, powers, and dominions.

Therefore, I cancel any and all demonic attacks and assignments against me, my family and my ministry in the name of Jesus. I reject any claims the enemy may make on me as I belong to the Lord Jesus Christ!

I declare myself free from the clutches of the enemy and put on the full armor of God as I take my stand against him. Jesus, thank you for my freedom!

Rebuking Lying Spirits

Lord, you said in your word that you are the way, the truth, and the life. You came to earth to bring us truth and declared that if we abide in your word, we would know truth and it would set us free. I receive that word and declare that I am free from the clutches of the enemy and his lying spirits.

By the authority of Jesus Christ and in his name, I bind all lying spirits and mute their voices. I rebuke those lying spirits and declare they have no further impact upon God's people. I loosed truth to go forth in the name of Jesus. I pray that eyes and ears will be opened to truth, and that your people will no longer be susceptible to the lies of the enemy and his deceptive practices.

In the name of Jesus, I cancel all assignments of the enemy to cause dissension and disorder in our churches, in our schools, in our businesses, and in our government through lies and deceptive practices. I declare that our legal systems will be just and impartial, and that our political parties will operate with truth and honesty. I stand on your word that says whatever I bind and loose on earth has already been bound and loosed in heaven.

Lord God, please give us hearts of integrity as we go forth living our daily lives and showing the love of Christ to all we come in contact with. May we be governed by your written word which you breathed on and gave us for teaching, rebuking, correcting, and training in righteousness (2 Tim. 3:16). That word has power to convict us when we are wrong so we can take the necessary steps to correct it.

May we always abide in agape love which never fails! In the name of Jesus, I pray, Amen.

Freedom in Christ Prayer

Heavenly Father, I confess there are areas in my life that I have not yet surrendered to you. Lord, please forgive me as I also forgive those who have hurt and caused me pain. I submit myself to you and all my inner most being to the light of the Holy Spirit to do a work of grace in me and to cleanse me of all unrighteousness.

By the power of the Holy Spirit and in the name of Jesus Christ, I bind the demonic spirit that is affecting me and command it to leave right now. I loose the healing power of Jesus to heal and restore all the damage that the enemy has done.

Thank you, Lord for forgiving and cleansing me! I proclaim that I am free from unforgiveness. I am free from fear, and from all addictions. I am free from self-indulgence and lust. I am free from distrust and anger. I am free from lying. I am healed, delivered and set free!

Thank you for your weapons of prayer, of praise, of fasting, of the word, of the blood, and the mighty name of Jesus. Your weapons of warfare have divine power to demolish strongholds.

Blessed be the name of the Lord, for you are my Savior, my Healer and my Deliverer. Amen and Hallelujah!

Prayers of Intercession

The Living Word

I thank you Jesus for being the Living Word! You were with God in the very beginning and as the Word, you are God! All things were created through you and apart from you nothing was created. You spoke the world into existence and one day came into that very world you created to dwell among us as a human being. You became the Living Word, the image of the unseen and invisible God. In you is life and your life brought life to everyone.

Lord, I ask that you forgive those who fail to recognize you as God, our Savior. Forgive those who believe you may have lived on earth but only as a prophet, and not the one who sacrificed his life to grant eternal life to all who believe. You are so much more than some can perceive. You are the one who shed your blood for our sins, the one who was resurrected from the dead; who was seen by many witnesses, who ascended into heaven and is now seated at the right hand of God the Father!

It is my prayer that you will have an encounter with those who do not know you or believe in you. Visit them in their dreams and visions. Make yourself known to them as the great "I AM," the God who is, who was, and who is to come! Open blind eyes to the truth of who you are, the Living Word who lived among us. You are the one who God anointed with the Holy Spirit and with power who went about healing all who were oppressed by the devil for God was with you. (Acts 10:38)

Thank you, Lord for the time you spent on earth demonstrating for believers how to live as kingdom people in a sinful world. May we always follow your example and do the things you did by the power of God the Holy Spirit.

I love you Lord and exalt your name. Your praise will continually be my mouth. Amen.

Praying the Promises

Lord, I speak the promise of your word that there would be an outpouring of your Spirit in the last days. You said, "*I will pour out my Spirit on all people. Your sons and daughters will prophesy, your old men will dream dreams, your young men will see visions. Even on my servants, both men and women, I will pour out my Spirit in those days (Joel 2:28-29).*

Lord God, for your honor and glory in all the earth, I call out to you to fulfill your word once again as you did with the early church and at various times in our history. Send the mighty wind of your grace and power in our midst. Release demonstrations of your great love as you have done in generations past. Send forth revival as you have never done before.

Pour out your Spirit on all people; young, old, female, male, those who know you and those who want to know you. Convict the world of sin so they will cry out "what must I do to be saved?" Lord of the harvest, please send out workers to gather in the harvest, for the harvest truly is plentiful but the workers are few (Matthew 9:37-38).

Dear Lord, please revive your Church so that we are doing the true work of the ministry that you called us to do. Prepare us for the outpouring of your Spirit by giving us praying spirits and humble hearts. Change us through the power of your love. Increase our faith so that we stay the course no matter how long it takes.

I thank you Lord, for hearing this prayer and granting this request. In the name of Jesus, I pray. Amen.

Let the People Praise You

Let the people praise you O Lord! Let all the people praise you! For the universe was formed at your command. You and you alone spoke the world into existence. You laid the foundation of the earth and determined its dimensions.

Let the people praise you O Lord! Let all the people praise you! For you called forth light and separated light from darkness and said it was good. You brought forth the sun, the moon and the stars to light up the sky.

Let the people praise you O Lord! Let all the people praise you! You called for dry land to appear and it was so. You kept the waters inside its boundaries when it came forth at your command.

Let the people praise you O Lord! Let all the people praise you! For you called forth vegetation and seed-bearing plants after their kind. You called forth sea creatures, birds of the air, and all types of land animals. You said it was good.

Let the people praise you O Lord! Let all the people praise you! For you said, let us make humankind in our image and according to our likeness; and let us give them dominion over all the sea creatures, birds and the land animals.

Let the people praise you O Lord! Let all the people praise you! For you indeed formed and breathed the breath of life into the human being and blessed them to be fruitful and multiply on the face of the earth.

Let the people praise you O Lord! Let all the people praise you! For you love and care for human beings because we are made a little lower than you and crowned with glory and honor. Let all the people praise you!

Prayer for Those in Ministry

Lord God, I pray that those in ministry will desire to seek after you and dwell in your sanctuary. May they boldly enter the throne room of grace and have full confidence in their prayers to you. Teach them to pray strategically to get the best results from their prayers.

Fill them with renewed joy. May all the trials and discouragements of this past season, and any hope deferred, be gone from them in Jesus' name. May their souls rejoice and prosper as they draw nearer to you.

Release and activate the gifts you have given them. May they realize they have Holy Spirit power to heal the sick, raise the dead, and cast out demons. Grant them a fresh anointing for victory over the demonic forces that would attempt to stop them in their ministry.

Give them wisdom and revelation in the knowledge of you. Help them to know and discern the times so they will make right decisions concerning their ministry. May they remove all distractions so they can clearly hear from you and move when and where you are moving. Give them your heart for the lost. Grant them the boldness to go into unknown territory to take back what the enemy has stolen.

Lord, bring forth in them a new expression of worship. Give them a heart for radical praise to you. May their praise be so exuberant that it will bind the strongman and cause him to flee! I thank you Lord for granting this prayer request. In Jesus' name, Amen.

Prayer for the Lost

Lord God, I come before you on behalf of those that are lost. Your word says you sent your son who came to seek and save those that are lost; and it is your desire that none should perish. Therefore, I pray that you lift the veil from their eyes so that they might see Jesus Christ clearly. Open their ears to hear the gospel; penetrate their hearts with your love.

In Jesus' name, I come against the stronghold of pride and deception in the unsaved person's life that blinds them to the light of the gospel and tells them they do not need Jesus in their life. Help them to see how much Jesus loves them and wants them to be saved. Lord, I ask that you spoil every scheme of satan and cancel every thought he plants in their minds to deceive them.

Holy Spirit, please hover all around the unsaved and the backslider; convicting them of their sinful condition and releasing love and forgiveness. May they realize they need Jesus in their heart and that he is the only one that can fill that empty void.

I ask that godly workers be sent out to share the love of Jesus and the message of the gospel to the unsaved. Help me to boldly proclaim your word to those I come in contact with. May doors be open for me to witness of your saving grace.

Prepare my heart so that I will demonstrate love for them as I open my mouth to share the gospel. Prepare their hearts to receive the truth that you love them and desire to save them. Lord of the harvest, I thank you for the souls that are coming into the kingdom. Amen

Prayer for our Country

Lord God, we cry out to you in our time of need because you are a caring and benevolent God who loves us despise our wandering ways. We are a country who has strayed far from you and are serving other gods. As a result, we are confused, disoriented, deceived, and are scattered like sheep without a shepherd.

We have lost our first love, that love of our true and living God, and we have lost our love of our neighbor. Father God, we ask that you reach out to us with your loving hand of mercy and bring us back to you. Open our hearts to embrace your love and then impart that love to our fellow human beings. Help us to see the good in each other and not be so quick to criticize. Knit our hearts together in brotherly love for each other.

We ask that you bless our political leaders with wisdom from heaven that is first pure, then peaceable, gentle, willing to yield, full of mercy and good fruits, and is without hypocrisy (James 3:17). Guard their tongues to speak and declare those things that are positive and uplifting and will reunite our country. Help all of us to see and fulfill the destiny that you have for us. Remind us that we are a country that is called to be a beacon to others, to offer liberty and justice for all!

Lord, we pray to you because you are the God of heaven and earth, the great and awesome God. We repent on behalf of our country, for how we have turned from you and sought-after other gods. Please forgive us of our sin and cleanse our hearts.

Let your ears be attentive to the prayers of these your saints. Heed our cry and turn our hearts back to you. Thank you for your mercy. In the name of Jesus, we pray this prayer.

Justice for All

Lord God, you know that in the United States of America, we pledge allegiance to our flag that ends with the following statement: *"With liberty and justice for all."* Unfortunately, justice for all still eludes us. It is yet to be achieved.

Your word says:

> You love justice and you do not forsake your saints. Psalm 37:28.
>
> Let justice run down like water and righteousness like a mighty stream. Amos 5:24
>
> Judges must never twist justice or show partiality. Deut. 16:19
>
> It is not right to acquit the guilty or deny justice to the innocent. Prov. 18:5
>
> Cursed is anyone who denies justice to foreigners, orphans, or widows. Deut. 27:19

Justice in our country has been denied again and again to the poor, to the disenfranchised and to the marginalized. Lord, we know that is not your desire, so we are confident it will be amended as we pray to you for righteous and honorable law officers, attorneys, judges, and jury members.

We pray that all appointed and elected adjudicators have no deep-seated loyalty to a particular political party, or bias toward certain ethic groups. Grant them wisdom from heaven so they may judge without partiality and without hypocrisy. Balance the scales so that the poor and the innocent are included in the justice for all.

Touch the hearts of those in power. Give them your love of justice and a desire to judge righteously as your word requires (Psalm 72:1-

2). May they realize that justice and fairness must be administered impartially to conform to your desire for the people. Lord God, what you require from us in outlined in Micah 6:8 and that is to "Do Justly, Love Mercy, and Walk Humbly with you." May we all be in submission to that word.

Thank you for hearing this prayer. Amen.

Prayer to Bless Mothers

Lord God, we lift up mothers to you and pray a special blessing for them. We thank you that you created mothers to be nurturers in the caring of their children. They are loving, kind, and sensitive. Thank you that they can also be strong when necessary. Continue to strengthen them to walk this journey of faith, looking to you for the help that they need.

Lord God, we pray especially for young, single mothers struggling to raise their children without the assistance of the fathers. Grant them grace to handle the job of mothering to the best of their ability, without demeaning the fathers in the eyes of the children. We pray that you will raise up godly male role models to assist and support them.

You told us in your word that we should honor our mothers and fathers that our days would be long on the earth. Remind us again and again that we are commanded to do this, even if circumstances tell us something different.

We pray for the salvation of mothers who have not yet given their life to you. Draw them to you. Lift the veil that is covering their eyes from the truth that Jesus loves them and died so they could be redeemed and have eternal life.

Mothers – may the Lord bless you and keep you, may he make his face to shine upon you and be gracious to you, may he turn his face toward you and give you peace (Num. 6:24). In Jesus name, Amen

Prayer to Bless Fathers

Lord God, we lift up fathers to you and pray a special blessing for them and over them. We thank you that you created fathers to be the protector, provider and strength for the family unit. Sanctify them in your word.

We are grateful for the fathers who are carrying out the responsibilities of father-hood. They are steady, dependable and are indeed a source of strength for their families. We thank you for them.

Lord, we call on you to do a mighty work in this earth in the life of the men who have fathered children before they were ready and unable or unwilling to be the father the child needed. Some of the fathers have strayed so far away that they are losing sight of their purpose in life and on the verge of giving up.

Lord, forgive them and give them another chance to get it right as you did with the prodigal son. You are the God of grace and it is grace they need. Holy Spirit, draw them to you! Give them a new heart and a new spirit and an openness to your promptings.

Turn the hearts of the fathers to the children and the hearts of the children to the fathers (Mal. 4:6). Bless them to be the kind of fathers you desire for your children; the kind who will put you first. Place people in their path who will encourage them in their walk with you; may they grow in maturity and wisdom.

Fathers – may the Lord bless you and keep you, may he make his face to shine upon you and be gracious to you, may he turn his face toward you and give you peace (Num. 6:24). In Jesus name, Amen

Prayer for Our Schools

In the name of Jesus Christ, we bind the demonic spirits over our schools and we tear down their strongholds using the mighty weapons God has provided us. We command the enemy to loose his hold upon the school systems in the name of Jesus! Free our children from the effects of every spirit of the occult, sexual immorality, all types of addictions (drugs, alcohol, pornography, nicotine) and idolatry. Lord, we release your ministering angels to go forth ousting the forces of darkness and evil.

We believe that the entrance of your word brings light and that you watch over your word to perform it. We pray that your word would enter the hearts of teachers and administrators, so that they will live the type of life that will bring you glory. We ask that the wicked be rooted out and those that remain will operate in godly wisdom and integrity.

Lord, we pray for the children and young people in the schools. Watch over them and keep them safe. Place someone in their path who will tell them about the love and forgiveness of Jesus Christ and his saving power. We ask that their hearts be made receptive to the hearing of the gospel. We also pray they will give themselves whole heartedly to their studies, learning all they can resulting in good grades.

We pray for the parents of the children that they will come to know you. Give them loving and patient hearts in raising their children. Bless them to be the best parents they can be. May their children's education be high on their list of priorities and grant them to know that a child's mind is being shaped under their watch.

We thank you that you are the delivering God. Thank you for intercessors who are praying for the schools and their occupants; and for laborers of the harvest to proclaim your word. Thank you for the victory. In the name of Jesus Christ, we pray. Amen.

Declarations
&
Decrees

Decree for Racial Unity in the Church

Father God, in the name of Jesus we declare that:

We are all created in your image. (Genesis 1:28)

We are all one in you. (John 17:20-21)

We are the body of Christ. (1 Cor. 12:4-11)

Jesus, you are the vine, we are the branches. (John 15:1-8)

The love in us is not mere words. (1 John 3:18)

We love you God, and we also love our neighbor (Matt. 22: 37-38).

Father God, even as we are created in your image, we decree that the eyes of our hearts are open to see each other as you see us. We are the sons and daughters of the true and living God.

We decree that the evil of racism finds no home or place in us. We work for justice and peace so that all barriers to your grace which oppresses our brothers and sisters will be removed.

We declare that forgiveness and reconciliation is our focus and goal. We reject racial stereo type slurs and jokes; we reject negative words spoken against each other and we decree a conversion of hearts and minds to the drawing of the Holy Spirit.

We thank you Lord that our strength of unity is derived from our diversity!

Baby Blessings and Declarations

Lord, you created this baby in their mother's womb; they are fearfully and wonderfully made, your works are wonderful. Your eyes saw their unformed body, and all the days ordained for them were written in your book before any of them came to be (Psalm 139:13-14, 16).

Before you formed this baby in the womb, you knew them and you have set them apart to do your work (Jer.1:5).

You said, "I know the plans I have for this baby, plans to prosper them and not to harm them; plans to give this baby a hope and a future (Jer. 29:11).

This baby dwells in the secret place of the Most High and is abiding under the shadow of the Almighty (Psalm 91:1).

The Most High is the dwelling place of this baby, so no harm or disaster will come upon them. For God will command his angels to guard this baby in all their ways. With long life will God satisfy and show this baby his salvation (Psalm 91:9-11, 16).

This baby is blessed in the city and blessed in the country — where ever this baby is, and where ever he or she go, they are blessed of the Lord (Deut. 28:3)

Declarations for Children/Grandchildren

Father, we thank you that your word is a sharp sword and a powerful weapon against satan. We declare and decree your word over our children and grandchildren. We declare that they have repentant hearts (Psalm 51:1-3), and that their lives bear the fruit of the Spirit (Gal. 5: 22-23). We declare and decree that they trust in you for direction and not lean on their own understanding (Prov. 3:5-6). They will live by the Spirit and not gratify their flesh (Gal. 5:16).

Lord, we declare and decree that our children/grandchildren walk in paths of righteousness for your name's sake, that they fear no evil for you are with them (Psalm 23:3-4). You have not given them a spirit of fear, but of power, love, and a sound mind (2 Tim. 1:7) We decree that they dwell in the house of the Lord all the days of their lives (Psalm 27:4).

We declare Lord, that they are obedient and honor their parents in the Lord that it may go well with them (Eph. 6:1-3). We decree that they have a humble heart to pray and seek your face (2 Chron. 7:14). Our children/grandchildren are taught of you Lord and great shall be their peace (Isaiah 54:13).

Our children/grandchildren are fearfully and wonderfully made, because your works are marvelous (Psalm 139:14).

Self-Declarations and Decrees

I declare and decree the following for myself because it is your word.

I declare and decree that:

I have a humble heart and a contrite spirit (Is. 57:15) and that I walk in humility before the Lord (James 4:10).

I have wisdom and revelation in the knowledge of God (Eph. 1:17).

I walk not after the flesh, but after the Spirit (Gal. 5:25).

I have a hunger and thirst for the Lord (Ps. 42:1) and desire to well in the Lord's presence all the days of my life (Ps. 27:4).

I delight in the word of the Lord and meditate on it day and night (Ps. 1:2).

I love the Lord with all my heart, soul, and mind and loves my neighbor as myself (Matt. 22:37, 39). I walk in the love described in 1 Cor. 13:4-7.

I am strong in the Lord and in the power of His might (Eph. 6:10).

I have on the full armor of God so that I can take my stand against the devil's schemes (Eph. 6:11).

I will not fear what man will do because no weapon formed against me will prosper, and any tongue that rises up against me in judgment is condemned (Is. 54:17).

Declarations and Decrees for Pastoral Leaders

We declare and decree the following over his/her life because it is your Word:

They have a humble heart and a contrite spirit (Is. 57:15).

They walk in humility before the Lord (James 4:10).

They have a spirit of wisdom and revelation in the knowledge of God (Eph. 1:17).

They walk not after the flesh, but after the Spirit (Gal. 5:25).

They have a hunger and thirst for the Lord (Ps. 42:1) and desires to dwell in the Lord's presence all the days of their life (Ps. 27:4).

They delight in the word of the Lord and meditates on it day and night (Ps. 1:2).

They love the Lord with all their heart, soul, and mind and loves their neighbor as themselves (Matt. 22:37, 39). They walk in the love described in 1 Cor. 13:4-7.

They are strong in the Lord and in the power of His might (Eph. 6:10).

They have on the full armor of God so that they can take their stand against the devil's schemes (Eph. 6:11).

They will not fear what man will do because no weapon formed against them will prosper, and any tongue that rises up against them in judgment is condemned (Is. 54:17).

Other books by Author
Audrey C. Jackson

Prayers for the Journey

The Church-Functioning in Miracles, Signs, and Wonders

Holy Spirit Study Guide

Spiritual Warfare Study Guide

Spiritual Authority of All Believers

Healing Through Deliverance

Discipleship Lessons for New Believers

All books are available at Amazon.com or you can contact the author by email worship29@verizon.net

Made in the USA
Middletown, DE
27 February 2023

25450357R00040